Letters to heaven ...

When days are long, and nights, e'en longer,
tis here I'll keep my words for you....

Copyright 2016

ISBN-13: 978-1530334421
ISBN-10: 153033442X

In another time....

As of late, I've had more than one opportunity to speak with friends, family, and others haunted by loss, by grief.

While grief is surely interest paid on having loved, it is still devastatingly difficult for most. The more we try to get beyond it, the slower the process becomes.

But on more than one occasion, I've recommended the starting of a journal, a keeper for both memory and recollection.

And there, the idea for this effort, to create a place of both honor and solace. Of intimacies, joy, and tears – shared again and new.

Love never leaves us.

Bobbie

Our days are spotted by loss and grief.........and a world of well-meaning people who pat us on the back and tell us 'everything will be okay'. And surely it will, but it will not be the same. I feel sad for the soul who doesn't understand – that some hurts aren't meant to scab over. I have lost many who I loved deeply, and I've yet to find any other person who could perfectly fit into the place left by another. It cannot be done, and it shouldn't be. Our healing isn't about getting us back to 'normal'; it's about learning how to live (to love) even when much of who we are seems to have been lost.

In times of great sorrow, my only joy seemed in the moments just after waking, a time when I could almost convince myself that it was all a dream. But over time, I found another joy – an almost secret knowledge – that I've not lost a one. I sit cross-legged on the floor with a cup of coffee by shear habit, a nature........and yet, my grandmother is there. I laugh and beneath the squealing pitch of a little girl, the timber that is my grandpa's voice. My granny lifts the cup to her lips, with pinkie extended just so........and more than once, I've felt the calm reassurance of my uncle's hand at the small of my back. Some store away treasure in cedar, but the real treasure is that which we carry – all who have loved us, in us, still.

If we know heartbreak, then we must also know love. If loss, then surely abundance. Joy sits many a night on the same bed as once we mourned. Our ability to hurt, to break, to fall......there are blessings unaware, reminders of the times we laughed, danced, and soared. Always, we are blessed. Let us not forget the letting in letting go.

what is now ....

we've come to find ....

endearing as the heart ....

to swell ....

as oceans ....

once a tear began ....

love returned ....

the soul to home ....

another life ....

to tell ....

....

....

....

....

....

....

....

....

of colors

remaining

as dust off the fields

the taste of a name

on our tongue

is proof of another –

(sometimes to recall)

blooms on the path

from a dream

we become

....

....

....

....

....

....

....

....

....

....

....

....

....

....

....

....

....

there are places   ....

untouched   ....

by the passing of time   ....

sorrows much deeper   ....

than grief   ....

a wanting for wisdom   ....

would alter our fate   ....

and take us to home   ....

on wings of belief   ....

....

....

....

....

....

....

....

....

....

....

....

....

....

....

to a life   ....

beyond living   ....

unremembered to sin   ....

held as a breath   ....

still blossoming there   ....

shaded by seasons   ....

restored us   ....

from death   ....

as memories held   ....

to the heart   ....

unaware   ....

....

....

Webster defines bliss as a state of extreme happiness, ecstasy or spiritual joy. Of all the words available, I'm almost certain that isn't a word that describes those dealing with loss, with grief. In fact, for most, it's just that – an imagined state just beyond our reach.

And yet, for a moment, let yourself imagine your loved one in such a place – a place of bliss.

It's quite comforting really, even if just for today.

Unfortunately, none of us know exactly what awaits us beyond death, but in many cases, the life and the end of this one was filled with pain, sorrow and loss. If you can't imagine the bliss, then imagine the loss of those burdens.

beyond
this winter of sorrow
she wakes in
eternal spring
she lives now -
she loves now

....

....

....

....

....

....

....

....

....

....

....

....

....

....

....

....

....

....

....

....

....

Photo

....

....

....

....

....

....

....

....

....

....

....
....
....
....
....
....
....

in seasons   ....

remaining   ....

as dust off the fields   ....

the taste of a name   ....

on our tongue   ....

is proof of another –   ....

(sometimes to recall)   ....

blooms on the path   ....

from a dream   ....

we become   ....

....
....

....

....

....

....

....

today
I thought of you
as tender eyes
met mine
and another
other muttered
her clothes never match
houndstooth
and leopard
aging westerns
leathers
the color of clay
a faint memory
of loving refrain
silver and shocking
how one can remember
the taste
of november
long past the rain

....

....

....

....

....

....

....

....

....

....

....

....

....

....

what name
was once you called to me
echoes o'er the storm
a distant light
unshaken by these memories
of home
a part of all that mattered
is forgiveness settled round
in tireless waves
the ways we were
before again abound
the sweetest blossoms
scattered
as breath in silence still
remains of wishes
traded
another place to fill
a lullaby forgotten
though not for comfort lent
as days I lost
ten thousand more between
counted from a distance
roads and stars
the same
paths converge
within the fault
of dreams

Yesterday afternoon, I spoke at length with a friend in California. It's been almost 30 years since I worked for her husband, George.

Two months ago, George stumbled while mowing the yard and subsequent check-ups found him suffering due to an inoperable tumor, brain cancer. He's not likely to make it through the week. But for a little while, we laughed and I shared stories of what a bear he was to work for at first. How could he have known he had met his match when he hired me, that his gruff exterior would be worn away by a girl with different beliefs and hand-me-down boots?

It seemed to fit. This past week has been a time of extreme tenderness for me. My father was moved to a hospital near to my house, where he stayed for more than a week as doctors worked to rid him of an infection that was not only hindering his healing, but negating his ability to communicate effectively about what was hurting. Whispers couldn't be interpreted and many a tear was shed over something that might have been nothing – words no one could understand.

And there was laughter as well – an evening when my father recognized neither me or my sister, and surely fell in love with both of us as we cared for his aches and washed his tired eyes.

Writing has been something on my mind, but left to the margin of most of my days. Early one morning, I scribbled on my hand as I sat upright beside my daddy's bed, listening to his breathing, my breathing….the same. But by the time I got home, the words were gone – worn to grey, and lost to the illusion of sleep.

Yet, I knew what I wanted to say, what I knew was mine to tell....that this is our treasure. These moments, regardless of how fragile they might seem, are the very threads that sew us together.

A well-meaning friend recently commented that when his father was ill, he had to 'limit' the time spent with him, and I wondered how in the world that was possible, and why in the world it would ever be a consideration. What blessings are negated for the comfort of a tv and a remote control......

Surely, we are always wishing for better days, for healing and hope and longevity. But at the heart of living is something deeper than what we know – that this one shining (glimmering) moment is divine, and all we have assurance of. We cannot expect even one more day or one more morning when the fish are biting and the air is cool, when the mourning doves scuttle across rusty tile, and truth shines through our window as bright as the day we were born.

So, when it comes, in clothes we do not recognize and eyes deeper than the sun is blue, let us not look away for even a moment. Let us never be fooled into believing that tears are anything less than glory, reminders of love we cannot lose, joys we have held closer than the stars.

This is our story, our forever, our inheritance. When all is gone, this is what we have. Time when nothing else mattered but the warmth of a hand in ours, lips that whispered our name, and the quiet still just before dawn.

This.........o, yes...........this!

....

....

....

....

....

Photo

....

....

....

....

....

....

....

....

....

....

....

....

....

silent ....

raindrops ....

will comfort me now ....

a hundred times – ....

of listening ....

volumes unconfessed ....

across a missing ....

separated – ....

mourning ....

words of love ....

....

....

....

....

....

....

....

....

Photo

· ·

· ·

· ·

· ·

· ·

· ·

· ·

· ·

fancy this
a truth divine
was never meant
for losing –
and somewhere still
the sea retreats
and never feels the sand

....

....

....

....

....

....

....

....

....

....

....

....

recalled as dew
– the comfort
of morn
as light unto shadows
I once I held you near
and pulled to the corners
the essence
of night
a blanket of secrets
tell me again
why the moon rises
to watch from afar –
and where go the wishes
when falling
for me

....

....

....

....

....

....

....

....

Photo

....

....

....

....

....

....

....

....

....

....

....
....
....
....
....
....
....
....
....
....
....

....

....

....

....

....

....

....

....

morning keeps
her secrets well
and no one knows to talk
of shadows come
and who is left
to say

passion wears
a flannel gown
and takes her comforts
slow

fingers trace
the memory
of stay

Photo

....

....

....

....

....

....

....

....

....

....

....

....

....

....

....

....

....

beneath
this tangled mess of scars
a map of miseries
a fortress built
of loneliness and pain
permission
has a silent voice
learned of lessons past
comfort found
in fears I know
by name

....

....

....

....

....

....

....

....

....

....

gather now
the aging wheat
and lay the seed aside
so that the sun
will dry
these tears again
tend our hearts
within the joy
we knew would come this way
mornings left us
sleeping
side by side

how could we then
have known of this –
of other blessings come
of stories yet untold
I listen now
to hear them mend
a tired soul
reminders of the road
miles before and someday
here I'll be

bless these willing hands
forgive me
let me take of all
I am

....

....

....

....

....

Photo

....

....

....

....

....

....

solace
wears a mask of grief
home – a time began
where reaching back
too often - I am found
mesmerized by everything
let my soul embrace
the tender touch
no matter now
how brief

sorrow
knows of other times
of joys too big
my heart to spare
of wonders
we shall know again –
bliss (o sweet)
forever shared

evening
sits in shadow
where once the morning sun
was burned
love remains
the proof of life –
beyond the still
a moment
yearned

··

··

··

··

··

··

··

··

··

··

··

··

not so many
miles from here
a road where none
is now
weaved of silver gazers
clementine
drinks from tides
the rain has left –
to comfort me
sometimes
of nights
I swear
I walk ten thousand
miles
to feel the cold
eternity
sweat against my skin
and wake the day
with mud between
my toes

....

....

....

....

....

....

of ways I've known
worn down by years –
and promises of time
to bring me home
the long way back –
don't need a map to know

the cool of dirt
beneath my feet –
rains to wash me clean
night birds sing to silence
swells beneath
the bone

....

....

....

....

....

....

....

....

....

....

....

....

....

....

....

....

....

....

Photo

stay
that I might tell you
of times before the fall
for prehistoric winters
might I grieve

the leaving
for the welcome back
poetry you wrote
lines returned
a promise to believe

verses of surrender
confession heard the same
as ancient constellations
to pretend

the path
was never easy
as getting back to one
a forest grew to block the view
again

held me here
one faraway
decision to return
across a sky of blue
another day

slipped
into the ocean
embrace of waking arms
as breezes come
to carry me
away

of a moment
I'm uncertain –
where choices came undone
days dissolved to years
so close –
this far

of somewhere else
forgotten by –
the distance worn between
will – no more forsaken
than the memory
of ways –

where huddled we
together
in the space
where secrets fell
trading lies
for mysteries
stories fitting still

to loving curves
shadows pulled away
by evermore
– murmurs
of redemption
echoes burning bright

warmth –
a fragile trading
of all we came
to love

....

....

....

....

....

....

....

....

....

....

....

....

somewhere else
kept just beyond
the places I recall
comes from time to time
a memory

Photo

....

....

....

....

....

....

....

....

....

once
in still
another wrote
his name
upon my soul
a lovely shade –
no different
than my own
cursive drew
across and through
back and forth
(remember)
the stiches were so small
I never knew

the almost lines
of future lives
the need
where grief would tarry
for never would
my story
love deny
dots and dips
and slashes –
longing curlicues'
are weaved
into the rhythm
of a sigh

....

....

....

....

Just this week, a friend told me of the start of a new tradition within her family wherein each member shared their best Christmas memory. Even in recounting the experience, tears filled her eyes as she spoke of her own, and those shared by others. There were moments of sorrow and others of pure joy, but eventually, they all became the best memory ever.

How is it that we've forgotten that? To know that every sorrow wears a coat of joy, and every bliss is but a warning of grief – a missing of the sweetest part? And yet, when measured into the same overflowing cup, they become the best – again and again.

She asked to my best memory ever and I think (partially) it was dislodged from my heart by her telling, but it is one of joy and family..........the best ever still.

Though we didn't know it at the time, we weren't rich. My family of six lived in a two bedroom trailer until I was twelve. Then we moved into a castle of three bedrooms….. :) The memory recalled is from the 'castle'. Every Saturday was the same. One by one, my brother and sisters would wake for some reason and make our way to my parent's room, my parent's bed. Until we were all there, telling our dreams, torturing and tickling, and eventually deciding on breakfast.

But Christmas was another such time. My brother (who by virtue of the fact that he was the only son, had his own bedroom) would sleep in the girl's room. We'd all pile into one big bed (or it seemed big at the time – tho I suspect it was no more than a full-size). I'm not sure we slept at all, but during the night, with every little squeak or bending of board, we'd speculate that Santa had come around. My brother was the designated outlook for us, and he would sneak down the hall to spy on the living room.........and then run back to the safety of us to report. There was no understanding that it had to be five o'clock before we could get up. The only restriction was that we couldn't get up before Santa had arrived.

Years later, I have heard stories of how long it took to get all the presents under the tree*. Between wrapping, assembling, and playing with all the toys – it was their joy we were most anticipating I think. Even now, at Christmas, I imagine the sound of little boy feet running down the hall........ 'he's here, he's here'...........

Let us keep Christmas forever in our tiny hearts, remembering things little as big. Let us keep love through the sharing of stories – creating anew every best memory.

* My Chatty Cathy doll was almost worn out before Christmas, and a promise to get a kitten for my sister resulted in an unexpected run to the country – and a cat that nearly brought my dad to stitches. In the telling, even more sweet beautiful tears. My dad comments, 'we didn't know just how good we had it'…. Then he winks, 'yeah, we knew'……..

....

....

wake me home
some other year –
beyond this life surrendered
fall to me the places
I have known –
save for me
a little room
with not much more
for leaving –
arms to fill
wake me now
to home

. .

....

....

....

....

....

....

....

....

of truth
the soul remembers
as falling
tears became
a promise made
– what more the light
might bring

settled down
these wantings –
of cedar planks and pine
songs are writ
to circles –
angels sing

back into
the starting
and who would blame
our grief
for seasons
thrice denied
the taking in

winter pulls
the shadowed moon
with longing
for the first –
willing only this –
to love again

....

....

....

....

....

....

....

....

....

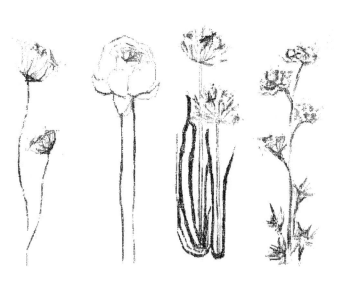

Photo

....

....

....

....

....

....

....

....

....

e'en now
I remember
a sliver of moon
and tiny white shells
on the ground
poems were written
each night
as I lay
neath a cradle of stars
– a heart without sound

....

....

....

....

....

....

....

....

....

....

reasons
and seasons
worthless regard
for the way
the rain sang
of the desert sometimes
telling anew
with words
scarcely heard
spent in beginning
a search
for the last
place we were almost
torn from the story
redeemed
by the memory
of none

. . .

....

....

....

....

....

....

....

....

....

....

....

....

....

Photo

were mornings come
a salve to ease
these passages of time
forgotten now
are distances between
the last hello
the first goodbye
melt into the day –
becoming but a memory
of dreams

....

....

....

....

....

....

....

....

....

....

....

....

....

....

....

....

....

....

....

....

before the truth awakens
prayers to silence fall
erasing years
outnumbered by the night
as destinies defended
to an ever faithful moon
love is gathered
sweetly
into light

. . .

she said
of times
unspoken –
was I first to hold you near
the last to kiss –
the last
to disappear

you wonder
when I wander –
how I wish
that you could know
there is nowhere I am going
you won't go

. . .

....

....

....

....

....

....

....

....

....

swept along
on lullabies –
sing me home
another
time we passed
of moments –
o so few

prayers awake
as secrets take
the heed
of my confession
to speak aloud
the poetry of trust

gather me
carry me –
will me now
to hurry
– my soul is freed
to wear the name
of love

....

....

....

....

....

....

even now
I wish
there were things
that you knew
of places I go
to wander the night
might you see
without sight
like ten thousand before
as spark to the empty –
a star beyond light

as a place
of beginning –
fields standing bare
with will for another
hurt to erase the memory of ruin
is burdened by grief –
by prayers
never heard –
unspoken to grace

would nature return
as the first
light was come –
without reason or want
for the falling into
a story awaiting
your hand at the pen
making truth of the darkness
what is seen –
what is knew

. . .

....

....

....

....

....

....

....

....

Photo

....

....

....

....

....

....

....

....

....

in a voice
as soft
my dreams become
a memory of
knowing
tho who can hear –
I speak
not loud enough
swept upon
a whisper – secrets
loosed by living
– song is poured
into the place
I love

. . .

....

....

....

....

....

....

....

....

....

letters
I've been writing
saved my name a place –
walked between my dreams
a mile with you
worried not
the path to choose
or what of time shall fill –

a story
meant for telling
kept for me
the end

. . .

49697912R00074

Made in the USA
Columbia, SC
26 January 2019